The Telemarketers' Hip-Pocket Guide to Opening and Closing *The Deal*

J. Everett Knight

Zen Boulevard

Published by Zen Boulevard, LLC
The Art of the Printed Word
Salt Lake City, Utah
All rights reserved.

Copyright © 2009 by James E Knight

First Edition Paperback May 2018

Printed int eh United States of America

ISBN: 1719145601

ISBN-13: **978-1719145602**

No part of this publication may be reproduced, stored in a retrieval system, or transmitted in any form or any means, electronic. Mechanical, photocopy, recording, or otherwise, without written permission from the author.

DEDICATION

To all sales people everywhere of all types for all things.
Nothing happens until it's sold.

And, God, but can it be a bitch, or what?

FORWARD

This is the ego page where I'm supposed to brag about my accomplishments to validate my experience and justify writing this little guide.

Ninety-Nine out of 100 readers will skip this self-serving intro to get right to the meat of the subject. And let's face it, you'll deduce whether I have the experience and know what I'm talking about or not, and that's only if you get enough out of it to improve your own production and raise your income.

Any and everything else is bullshit.

However, this little guide is not an esoteric tome on the psychological facets of telemarketing for the purpose of giving advice. Its purpose is for you to understand the sales *process*, that step-by-step procedure we all use to convince someone to do anything. You can dissect and catalogue a multi-million-dollar contract into specific steps leading from the beginning to the end; the initial contact to the close; from the first words of introduction to the wedding; from the first contact with a prospect to closing the deal.

Each phase has its own steps and after a while I developed my own rules. I provide them here as guidance only.

Along the way you will undoubtedly develop your own style around your own rules, and that's even better. Do what is right for you. The rules I operate under are listed at the back of this guide. Take what works for you and piss on the rest.

The examples I provide are based on my years of telemarketing experience, and are purposely exaggerated to illustrate a point. The idea is to demonstrate the information you have to get from the prospect, and then how best to use it in order to control the sale to the close. It's the *Action of Obtaining and Managing Information* that's important in each stage, how you get it depends on you and your own style.

You are a telemarketer, or a salesman of any kind, and it is your job to convince others to buy your product because you profoundly believe it is the best thing your prospect can do for themselves, and it's your job to get the prospect to believe it, too. You've worked hard, and in some, if not many cases very long, and you don't get paid unless someone buys what you have to sell. And, by God, the object is to make *money*. The process is simple, getting paid is just another part of it.

The best advice anyone ever gave me was to just *Be Me*. We all have our own style in everything we do in our lives, don't think you have to be something or someone different in order to be successful. You don't. If you do, the prospect will perceive it, know you're full of crap and won't do business with you.

Don't pitch, don't perform . . . ***COMMUNICATE*** Put your feet up, let your hair down, and talk like you would to an old friend. Be yourself, use your own style. Don't worry about the sale, just go through the process, have fun, make a new friend along the way, and the sale will take care of itself.

Table of Contents

FORWARD..i

The Magic of Telemarketing...1

PHASE I Opening/Introduction..4

PHASE II The Presentation..14

PHASE III Handling Objections...18

Seven Steps to Overcoming Objections 22

PHASE IV The Close 26

The Most Powerful Question in the Close............................29

PHASE V Follow Up...32

Sixteen General Rules Of The Sales Process........................34

The Magic of Telemarketing

Some people object to the weather and others disagree with the government. You can bet everyone will disagree with you about something sometime just as others will object to buying your product. This does not mean that the prospect is not interested, nor does it mean he will not buy. The prospect undoubtedly bought similar products to yours in the past, which means he will most likely buy them again in the future.

So many times a salesperson will flub for nothing more simple than not having grasped the sales *process*. With that, a telemarketer, or sales rep of any kind, can exercise more control and provide the prospect with sufficient reason to buy *NOW!* That requires knowledge of the process and knowingly going through each step. It requires knowledge of your product(s), **Knowledge of the Competition** (notice the emphasis), and understanding why people object to buying anything.

One of the most important things to remember, above and beyond anything else, is this:

Rule #1
No One Sells Everybody Everything Every Time

Repeat that: *No one sells everybody everything every time.* The object is to reach as many people as you can, then through training and experience, sell a higher percentage of those you do contact.

Standardize your presentation, perfect a given course and *don't deviate from it*. Don't pitch one way to Bob, and then pitch another way to Fred. And never take a sales rejection personally; it will kill you.

Depending on your product, an average telemarketer should close 10-20 percent of *contacts* he makes. Meaning on average, for every ten people you find to pitch your product, six will flatly say **"NO!,"** four will say "Maybe," and then depending on how well you handle their objections and control their fear, one or two will say "Ok. I'll take it." Even a multi-million dollar producer doesn't sell everyone he contacts. It's in the numbers; the more prospects you contact, the more you will sell. And the better you get at the process, the higher closing ratios you'll have. Nothing mysterious about that. This is a general rule, so of course there will be any number of exceptions depending on the product you're selling and the client base you develop.

Nevertheless, consider this a law of the universe: No matter how bad or inexperienced a salesperson you are, if you talk to enough people, sooner or later someone will roll right over and say, "Ok. I'll take it." It's happened to every salesperson I've known, and that's a lot. It happens to everybody. It's happened to me. It will happen to you, too.

It is also persistence. The more you stay in the prospect's mind, the more likely he will purchase your product. In this sense, "The squeaky wheel gets the grease" is quite right. However, know the difference between persistence and being a pest. Set your own limit on how much you'll persist with one prospect. Persisting doesn't mean he'll buy, but it can mean he will when others won't. If for every month in a year a particular salesperson calls a particular prospect, sooner or later that prospect will buy--fact of life.

Rule #2
Sales Is The *Process* Resulting In The Close *Not The Event Of The Close Itself*

I believe this point of view is critical. Sales *is* a process, definitive steps leading to a specific objective–the close. Perfecting your delivery will bring a greater degree of control and result in a higher closing ratio.

I Break the SALES PROCESS into five steps:

Step I –Opening / Qualifying
Step II -- Product Presentation
Step III -- Handling Objections
Step IV -- Close
Step V - Follow-up, Customer Service

Let's see how each phase and how it all flows together.

PHASE I
Opening/Introduction

THE TELEPHONE! The greatest invention since sex. You can contact a hundred people in one day using the telephone, whereas only a fraction of those in person. I'm referring to cold calling, drumming up new prospects, new accounts -- *Playing the Numbers*. The telephone is the single most terrific money-making tool there is.

There are Seven Crucial Aspects to consider when first contacting a prospect over the phone. They are:

1. Voice - Emotional state
2. Avoid Meaningless Clichés - Be *Different*
3. Be Concise
4. Explain and Get His Agreement
5. Qualify
6. Verify and Lock it
7. Make a New Friend

1.) VOICE – EMOTIONAL TONE

Many consider the telephone an impersonal instrument. Prospects do not see flesh and blood, open body language, sincere eyes, and a charming smile. They hear only a voice. But the voice carries the same inflections, tones and mannerisms the same as or even more than body language.

Rule #3
It's Not What You Say, It's *How* You Say It.

C'mon . . . Who hasn't had a lover's quarrel when that little dig was thrown in our face? "It's not what you said, it's *how* you said it!"

The "color" of voice indicates an emotional state, an attitude, a subliminal "tone" upon which a person views the world. Are they apathetic? Fearful? Angry? Antagonistic? Bored? Enthused? No matter how well you think you can cover up a low emotional tone, the subconscious recognizes it as clearly as if displayed on a neon billboard. If you're having a bad day, are angry about something, no matter how much you try to cover it with fake enthusiasm, the prospect will subliminally detect it. Do whatever it takes to be upbeat. Take a walk. Mentally prepare yourself by whichever way suits you best.

More important: Listen for the prospect's emotional state. Is he apathetic? Bored? Rushed? Impatient? Antagonistic? The more you listen for an emotional tone the more easier it is to spot. Read body language through tone of voice, and then present yourself in the *identical* tone. When there is anger in his voice (he's been having a bad day?) put a little anger in yours. *Identify* with him.

The prospect's tone will then rise to a point where he will be more receptive and *want* to contribute more to the discussion.

Rule #4
Matching The Prospect's Emotional Tone Will Raise His Tone To A Higher, More Receptive Level.

Be polite. Don't be intimidated. Talk to him the same way you would to a friend over drinks at happy hour. Be you--be normal. Have a good time. Don't sell a prospect, offer an opportunity to a friend. AT&T once said it best: The most important business calls *are* personal.

2.) Forget Dumb Clichés – Be Direct -- Be Different
"Good morning, Mr. Jones, Rob Smith from ABC Securities. ***HOW ARE YOU TODAY?***"

Ohhhhh, come onnnn. I cringe whenever I answer the phone and a telemarketer opens with that line. Rob Smith doesn't care how Mr. Jones is today. That opening has evolved into such a meaningless and insincere cliché it *warns* the prospect of an impending sales pitch. It's a shallow, disingenuous platitude. "How are you today?" identifies you as a salesperson. "Uh oh, this guy is a *salesperson*!" Lock and load, let loose the dogs, call in the 82nd Airborne.

"Man the battlements, men! Hide the checkbook! There's a salesperson is at the gate!"
"How do you know it's a salesperson, sir?"

"Because he asked me how I was today!"

Be direct – Be different: "Good morning, Mr. Jones. My name is John Smith from XYZ Securities. I know you're a busy man, so the last thing I'll do is waste your time. . ."

It doesn't matter *what* you say, it's the *intention behind* what you say. Don't sugar-coat it, kid, tell it like it is, but in your own way, use your own style. But ***BE DIFFERENT***, precise. Stick out from the crowd. What deviates from the norm is what commands attention and thus stimulates curiosity. By being different, the prospect will be more inclined to listen to what you have to say.

3) Be Concise!

I can't stress enough how important this is. This is the first contact, where you create the first and lasting impression. How you present yourself is how the prospect will visualize you, your company, and whether he'll keep listening or not. Be confident, be concise. When you first reach your contact on the telephone, and after the initial introduction:

Rule #5

Present Yourself, Your Company, Your Product And What It You Can Do For The Prospect Within *30 Seconds*.

The average person's attention span is no more than 15-30 seconds after the initial opening introduction. It's imperative to be direct and to the point.

"Good morning, Mr. Jones. My name is John Smith from XYZ Securities. I know you're a busy man, so the last thing I'll do is waste your time.

It's come to my attention you've participated in various investment opportunities in the past, and my company just come across an extraordinary vehicle with tremendous promise. If you have a quick moment, allow me to tell you about it and the potential returns, and then determine whether or not it would fit in your portfolio. May I have a few seconds of your time?"

Cut and Dried!

PLUS you're asking for his permission.

He'll either say "Go ahead" or "Not interested." If he's not interested, always acknowledge with a "Thank You, have a great day," and call somebody else. If he says, "Go ahead. . ."

4) Within *60 Seconds*, Describe Your Product or Service And How Your Prospect Can Benefit From It – And Then Get His Agreement.

". . . Mr. Jones, XYZ became a partner in a series of oil and gas re-entry projects. This means we're going back into old and at one time producing wells and bringing them back online into production. We project a three year breakeven point, and anywhere from fifteen to a twenty year production life. That sort of return on a relatively low-risk investment would be a great fit in anyone's portfolio, wouldn't you agree?"

Get the prospect to agree. In this case, the product is high returns on a low risk investment. And let's face it, there's room for improvement in everything we do. Nothing is ever perfect. Not the prospect. Not you. Not even me. Really.

5) Qualify

Does he have the money? Can he afford it? Will the anxiety of having invested money keep him awake at night?

There are two very strong reasons for this:

    a) You're not in the entertainment business. Develop relationships only with those who can afford your product. Save yourself a lot of time, aggravation and heartache, and,

    b) When he says he can't afford it later (and he will) when handling his objections, you'll know it's complete bullshit; just a meaningless attempt to catch the buying impulse. It won't be the real "WHY" behind his impulse to not buy, and it's also a tip-off that he is *about* to buy.

"Mr. Jones, XYZ is retaining forty percent of the working interest after the initial twenty percent royalty interest. We're offering the remaining forty percent in five percent blocks at $10,000 each. A ten thousand dollar investment is well within your comfort range, isn't it?"

If you tell a prospect what it "costs," he'll be thinking in the red. If you tell him how much he'll have to "spend," he'll still think of going in the red. Telling him it's an "investment," gets him thinking of returns--in the black.

If he says it isn't within his comfort zone, thank him for his time, promise to check on him in the future and call someone else – OR – find the level with which he is comfortable.

If he says it would be no problem:

6) Verify And Lock It!
"In other words, Bob (Notice we're now on *a first name basis*), a ten thousand dollar investment won't keep you awake at night? That's an easy amount for you to handle?"

Reaffirming this point will completely obliterate any "Money" objection later on.

7) Does He/Can He Make His Own Decisions?
Is he the decision maker? If he is, can he make the decision on his

own? Or does he consult with another authority, like an accountant or attorney or sheep's guts or Tarot Cards? You waste a lot of time and effort when dealing with those who can't make their own decision to buy anything–even their own underwear.

> "I take it then, Bob, you make your own investment decisions?"

If he doesn't, who does? What are their names? What are their relationships to him? Many consult with others, but still exercise the final decision. With whom does he consult? What relationship do they have?

HOWEVER, I, myself, and personally learned to not ever bother with those who consult with others, as it gives the prospect an easy excuse to say, "No." i.e. "I gotta check with my accountant" – or "attorney" or "goat's guts." Ok. What does an accountant or attorney or goats' guts know that the prospect doesn't? See my point?

Remember, now you're on a first name basis. Timing is everything. He knows who you are, what you do, where you're from and what you're offering. You know he's invested in the past, was interested or impressed enough to tell you he can handle a $10,000 investment with no problem and nobody else makes decisions for him. So now is the time for the subtle shift to the first name, and you want to be on a first name basis with a guy like that anyway. Right?

8) Make A New Friend

If you've followed the above steps effectively, you've been on the phone with him for only about a couple of minutes, maybe two minutes at the most. He *respects* the way you've presented yourself. He wants to expand his investment portfolio's (or whatever) performance. He makes his own decisions and can afford it. Now let your hair down, put your feet up, and chew the fat a while.

> How long has he been in his business?
> How did he happen to get into it?
> What other ventures/products has he invested/bought in the past?
> How well have they performed?
> Is he married?
> Kids? Boys? Girls?
> Other interests?
> You get the idea.

EXAMPLE INTRO CALL (using advertising):

Good morning, Mr. Jones, my name is John Doe, with XYZ publications.
> **(Avoid clichés - be direct)**

I know you're a very busy man so I'm not going to waste your time, but I see that you've been doing quite a bit of advertising lately, right?

(Be concise)

Mr. Jones, since XYZ increased our distribution channels, we've designed a new advertising campaign that will allow you to substantially expand awareness of your company to your target audience while lowering your costs. I know you've advertised in XX, and also YY *(he did his homework)*. My publication will reach a 25% larger audience while reducing your advertising costs by as much as 15%.

(Get agreement)

If even the remotest chance existed that I could prove my claim, it would be worth taking a look, wouldn't it?

(Qualify)

Terrific! Expanding your advertising channels would certainly improve your business, right?

(Verify and Lock it)

In other words, *(First Name)*, investing in your business by expanding your advertising campaigns at a lower cost will be no problem for you?

(Decision maker?)

(First Name), are your advertising procurements final? Or are there others who will contribute to the final decision? *(Who are they?!)*

(Get to know him)

I see you live in the Ritz section of town, (first name), right by Walk-Your-Dog Park, isn't it? Do you have any kids

PHASE II
The Presentation

There's the old saying: "You can lead a horse to water but you can't make it drink." Well, you're a salesperson, dummy, so remember--your job is not to lead prospects to water and make them drink--*Your job is to make them **THIRSTY!***

Rule #6
Standardize Your Presentation And The Way You Present It.

1) Do Your Homework - Know The Competition
What other comparable publications or investments or widgets are out there? Who's offering them? What are the advantages of the competition? Their weaknesses? Never offer the competition's advantages, ONLY the weaknesses. And *never knock the competition*, build yourself up. Politicians are the perfect example of what NOT to do. They spend more time slinging dirt on their opponents than in selling their own virtues. But, hey, they're politicians. As it is, you can't trust any of them. With prospects, it's an inherent and instinctive turnoff, and they won't trust you. Anyway, the more you talk of the competition, is all the more the prospect will think of them instead of you.

2) Be Prepared - Know Your Product
"I don't have a product. I have a service."

This argument is completely false. The result of your service *is* the product. What's the product of a carpet cleaning service? Clean Carpets. Of a financial planner? Secure and growing assets. Sell the result of your service, *that's* your product. With machinery, it's not what the machinery *is or has,* but what it can *do*. Does a manufacturer want 1/4" drill bits? Or does he want a bit that can drill a million clean, burr-less 1/4" holes?

Standardize your presentation to best demonstrate your products features, functions and benefits, and how each will benefit the prospect, and *don't deviate from it*. Don't get the idea that it has to be presented one way to Mr. Jones and another way to Mr. Smith.

Rule #7
The More Standard Your Presentation, The More Efficient the Delivery And The More Control You Have While Presenting It.

3) **Feature - Function - Benefit**

Know what you are going to say, why and how. What makes your product better for your prospect than others? Present the advantages the client will gain by using your product, more than the disadvantages of the competition. Praise your company and products, never degrade the competition.

Example of feature - function - benefit (using equipment).

Feature: "This is the chrome, reversed throw-up-thing-a-ma-jig, available only on XYZ Machinery."

Function: "It engages the chrome reverse mechanism to interact with the sling valve."

Benefit: "It operates by depressing a simple foot plate located at the bottom of the front panel. This design offers a more precise analysis of raw material uniformity than can be provided by any other machine, at a greater speed and with superior safety.

"I noticed your accident rate was pretty high on ABC's machines (he did his homework!). By engaging the mechanism with a foot plate, the operator's hands are kept away from the open machinery itself. It also engages more quickly and efficiently. With this feature, you can increase your output with improved quality and greatly reduce accident rates, and therefore production increases resulting in higher employee moral. Makes sense, doesn't it?"

4) Take Control

Without control of the presentation, you have no presentation. Do not be disrupted by questions or activities.

If the prospect has a legitimate question pertaining to what you are presenting at the time, answer it, then go back to where you were and continue. If he has a question pertaining to something not yet covered, acknowledge it, state that you are just about to cover that point, maintain where you are in the presentation, and continue.

"That's a very good question, Bob, and it pertains to a point I'm just about to cover."

Remember the question! Write it down if you have to. So when you do enter that part of the presentation, you can refer to it.

"Now pertaining to your earlier question about the new high yield bonds, this is where it ties into the overall picture . . ."

If activity takes his attention away from your presentation . . . **STOP!** . . . and *wait for him to ask you to continue*. Then back up to where you were just before the interruption and continue.

Again, be concise. **FEATURE - FUNCTION - BENEFIT** The more concise, the more you control the situation.

PHASE III
Handling Objections

Ninety percent of salespeople don't understand that handling objections is just another part of the process, and in itself has its own steps to follow. There isn't a salesperson anywhere that wasn't confronted at one time or another with an objection to which he had no idea how to respond. They froze, wracking their brain for some way not to look like a complete fool, to sound convincing and get the prospect back on track. Many salespeople cringe when faced with objections. They choke worse here than at the close. It is not necessary. One reason for this is taking an objection personally, and attempt to handle each objection off the cuff.

Rule #8
The Sale Doesn't Begin Until The First Objection Is Made!

It may sound trite but true. So far, you've done everything just right. You followed all the steps in the opening, in the presentation and delivered it well. Now the prospect is going to try to hold you off. Everything beforehand was the *presentation*, now comes the *sale*. Many salespeople, particularly new ones, use their imagination to satisfy the objections of their prospect without having any understanding of the psychology behind objections, nor of the proven steps to follow that can overcome them.

Why do prospects object to buying?

F-E-A-R

They're afraid of making the wrong decision. They're afraid of spending money. They're afraid of you. Why? Because you're a salesperson, dummy. A **_SALESPERSON!_** You're the enemy. You're convincing him to spend money. You're the devil of temptation making him WANT to spend money whether he thinks he should or not, or whether he even *has* it or not. WHY? Because you made him *THIRSTY*.

Rule #9

Fear Is The Motivating Factor Behind Every Objection To Buy

Do not confuse an objection for a condition. A condition is a legitimate reason why a prospect cannot buy. Bankruptcy, fire, IRS investigation, sudden death of partner or principal, soon retiring -- these are all conditions. You will never overcome a condition. Don't even try. But if you handled the opening properly in the beginning, you wouldn't have gotten that far anyway, right?

The Four Categories

There are as many objections to buying as products to sell, but they all come under just four categories:

1. **NO MONEY** (too much money, not liquid, can't afford it).
2. **NO HURRY** (maybe later, want to think about it, talk to friend,

CPA or attorney).

3. **NOT INTERESTED** (lack of confidence in you or your company).

4. **NO NEED** (can't use it, won't do me any good).

An objection is not a condition. An objection is always: A STATEMENT PRESENTING REASONS WHY THE PROSPECT FEELS HE CAN'T OR SHOULD NOT BUY.

> "I'll think about it"
>
> "I need to talk to my accountant"

These are objections, not conditions. They require statements that lead to the close. In most cases, *the response to an objection is not an answer but a question.*

Most people who raise objections are simply admitting they are apt to buy or at least CAN be sold. The objection is merely a lame attempt to check the buying impulse out of FEAR. Once you properly answer rebuttals, there is nothing left but to close the sale.

Rule #10
The First Objection Is Never True.

All of us at one time or another have been on the brink of buying something we knew we could do without or didn't need but ignored our "I should know better" instinct, and bought it anyway. When we did struggle with ourselves, it is surprising how we tried to slow a salesperson by putting up barriers to give us more time to think about it. It is even more surprising that, even though we had no malice, we blatantly lied through our teeth. Consider the last time you considered buying a car. You may not have been aware of it, but the odds are that sometime you instinctively resisted the salesperson, objected to having your name put on the bottom line. That's normal enough, but it may surprise you at *how* you objected. The man with $500,000 cash in the bank says "I can't afford it," while the man with a broken down clunker says he "doesn't need it."

In reality, the objection is just an attempt to counteract the logic of the presentation: a defense mechanism unconsciously triggered to hold off the seller. It will not remain a roadblock to the sale if the salesperson understands the human factor motivating the objection—FEAR--and methodically eliminates the bricks in the wall supporting that emotion.

A small percentage of objection handlers are excellent, but the overwhelming majority are mediocre and totally ineffective. An experienced salesperson will do better than most, but time and habit can produce repetitious, tired and worn closing clichés of which most reps are usually not consciously aware. Most will do the best they can under the circumstances, but this is often not good enough.

Although you can be taught the techniques of how to overcome objections and close the sale, you must have the hunger, desire and enthusiastic determination to persist. You must maintain the mental attitude that you will not, ever, accept a "No" because your attitude is one of helping the prospect, and how can any sane man say "No" to that?

Seven Steps to Overcoming Objections

There are seven steps to handling objections. These are:

1. Categorize
2. Acknowledge and Empathize
3. Feed Back and Clarify
4. Isolate
5. Respond and Hype
6. Test
7. Close

1. CATEGORIZE

Which objection is it - No interest, No need, No rush, or No money?

> "Well, before I do anything I have to talk with my accountant."

Hmmmm, he wants more time. This is a `No Rush' objection.

2. Acknowledge and Empathize

Let him know that you heard and understood what he said. *Acknowledge him.* It tells the prospect that you are listening to him, that what he has to say is important. It grants him identity. In an extreme example, imagine talking to someone who never looked at you, nor even said "yes" or "no" to basic questions. It's like you don't exist.

Empathizing is understanding his concern -- relating to it. In a way you're saying that you've been around that block too, and, yeah, it's a bitch, isn't it, Bob?

Acknowledge what he says, let him know that he exists and that what he says is important.
Empathize with him, let him know you understand his concern.

"Ok, Bob (acknowledgment), I know what you're saying and, boy, but can I ever relate to that . . . (empathize)"

Or

"Thank you for telling me that Bob (acknowledgment), I understand exactly what you're saying . . . (empathize)"

3. Feed Back and Clarify

Confirm what his concern is, then clarify this concern to your advantage. For instance, Bob wants to check with his accountant. OK, then assume he is saying he wants to buy what you're selling, but needs to check his finances.

"If I understand you correctly, you're saying you see the potential of our oil and gas re-entry projects, but you just need to figure the finances to participate, right?"

What else could an accountant tell him?

4. Isolate

This step is extremely important. It will tell you whether it is a legitimate consideration (that still needs handling) or just another lie to keep you at bay.

"So, what you're saying, Bob, is if the financing weren't a problem, I can count on you for a five percent interest?"

5. Respond and Hype

Deal with the issue and reinforce a benefit.

"Bob, accountants are very important, but in all my years I've never met a businessman who didn't know the state of his own finances. With a three year payout and up to a twenty year production life, you're accountant would think you crazy if you didn't do it."

6. Test

"Bob, at five percent each, only eight blocks are available. This is an extremely limited offering, and we plan to have the well back online within thirty days."

7. **Close**

"Then you need to help me get you started. This is what we hae to do . . . ."

All objections should be handled within the seven step format, and reference requests are no exception. When he asks for a reference, he's giving you a "No Interest" and/or "No Rush." In other words, he isn't yet sold and/or you have not sold him on doing it *now*. But a reference question could be very legitimate. He may really want to buy your product, but needs an outside referral to make him feel more secure in doing business with you. It also reinforces the isolation step of handling it. So:

"Bob, I'm certainly not going to refer anyone that didn't come out way in the black. However, if I do and you are 100% satisfied, I can then count on your participation, right?

> my system integrates with and enhances yours, making it more user-friendly for less cost and manpower, would I have a new Client?"

Prospect

> "Absolutely"

Salesperson

> Of Course. Let's conference with your tech manager and we'll get his assurance.

PHASE IV
The Close

Nothing happens until the sale is made. Closing is exactly that, it's closing the deal so you can move on and open a new one. Even the best sales people lose confidence and choke at this stage. They expect the prospect to make up his own mind to buy, because the salesperson made such a spectacular, convincing sales presentation.

WRONG!

1.   Ask For The Deal

You, the salesperson, have led him to the obvious conclusion to buy your product. You, the salesperson, have been controlling the transaction all along.

Rule #13
The Hardest Part Of The Process Is Making The Presentation, *Not Asking For The Deal.*

You did your homework. You were prepared. You presented everything flawlessly. You answered his questions perfectly without being flustered. You handled all the objections. You just did a lot of work and confronted a stressful business transaction all on your own that 99% of the people in the business world are simply unable to do. **We, as salespeople, are the ones that** *make things happen.* **Everyone else pushes our paper**. So what the hell is so hard about putting out your hand with a big, determined smile on your face and saying simply, "OK, Bob, let's do business."

Example:

"So, Bob, you see how my product will increase your production and lower your costs? Great! Because that's exactly what it will do. Now, I can be set up immediately and you'll be realizing the rewards just as quickly. So, let's get started right away."

THEN SHUT THE HELL UP!

2. **Handle The Objection**

Prospect: "Well, uh, I'm gonna hafta check a couple 'a things out first"

Salesperson: "Ok, Bob, I understand what you're saying. A lot of my customers have felt the same way, but they're using XWZ publications more than ever now. Tell me, Bob, what *exactly* is it that's holding you back?"

Prospect: "Uh, I want my manager to take a look at it."

Salesperson: Hmmmm:

a. **Categorize** - No hurry

b. **Acknowledge and Empathize** - "OK, Bob, I appreciate that"

c. **Feed Back and Clarify** - "You want to advertise in my publication, but you also have to respect your manager's position."

d. **Isolate** - "Is that the only thing that's holding us back for doing business?

e. **Respond and Hype** - "When your manager sees how busy he'll be with the increase in business, he's going to wonder why you haven't advertised with us long ago."

f. **Test** - "When your manager approves the specs will I have a new customer?"g. **Close**

3. If Necessary *REPEAT 1 and 2*

Rule #14
Choking At The Close Is Going Into Agreement With The Prospects Own Fear.

You just gave him power and control over *you*.

Rule #15
You'll Never Get The Deal Unless You Ask For It.

It's very true. What do you have to lose?

Prospects can smell need, they can sense desperation. You can't let them see you sweat, even if the life of your child depended on that sale. If they sense you're desperate, they'll lose all confidence in you *and* your company *and* your product—and walk.

Lack of confidence is a request for leadership. If you can't lead them to the sale, they'll lead you to the door.

Don't choke at the close. It's unnecessary. What's the absolute worst that can happen? He'll throw another objection at you to handle. You haven't sold him yet, is all.

You worked real hard to get there, and now you want to be *paid* for it. You must expect it. That's fair, isn't it?

The Most Powerful Question in the Close

When handling objections, notice that the objections themselves are as varied as the clouds. What you have to find is the common denominator of all his objections, which is the **REAL OBJECTION**. All the others were bricks in the wall protecting his buying impulse. But that wall has a foundation, and that foundation is the **Real WHY** behind his not moving forward now. Once that *real why* is found, you can handle it and close the deal. How do you find that? By asking the most powerful–and obvious-- question:

"What *EXACTLY* is it that's holding you back?"

Example:

    Used in Step #4, the Isolation stage:

Salesperson:

    "Bob, if financing wasn't a problem, would I have a new customer?"

Prospect:

    "Well, uh, maybe. I'd still have to consider some things."

He's still not yet closed- what does he have to consider?

Salesperson:

    "Thank you for telling me that, Bob, I can relate to what you're saying. (Be concise, but talk to a friend) Tell me something, Bob, ***What* exactly *is it that's holding you back?"***

Don't ask what he has to consider – he'll just make up something else. Ask for the ***REAL WHY.***

By saying he needed to consider some things, he's really saying "I'm not convinced." Why? So what is it *exactly* that's holding him back? What's the ***REAL WHY?***

Rule #11

Shut Up And Listen!

"What exactly is it that's holding you back?"

Rule #12

He Who Talks First Loses. Wait For The Prospect To Answer, Even If It Takes Until The Next Tuesday.

Salespeople can talk themselves right out of the deal. By talking more than listening, you're giving him ammunition to use against *you*. This is a sign of a salesperson's own fear, a lack of confidence. He's afraid to hear that the prospect won't buy so he never gives him the chance to say he *will* buy. Without getting an objection, there's no way to handle it, no way to close the deal. Keeping your mouth shut and listening enforces your control.

So, what is it ***EXACTLY*** that's holding him back? That's the one brick upon which his whole defensive wall is built. Find that ***REAL WHY*** brick, pull it out, and the whole wall will crumble. So, what is it *exactly* that's holding him back?

PHASE V
Follow Up

Follow-up after making the sale is just as important as making the sale in the first place. Follow-up is SERVICING the customer. Here is where you establish a strong rapport between you and the prospect for future business and referrals.

1.   **Schedule**

There is a good schedule to keep when following up:
Call the day after the close and ensure him you are right on top of things.

Call every other day for a week after he has had your product. If there are any problems, **HANDLE THEM IMMEDIATELY**.

Call at least once a week thereafter for one to two months. If there are ever any problems HANDLE THEM IMMEDIATELY.
Call once a month thereafter. Get referrals.

2.   **Rapport**

Don't try to sell him something every time you call. Build the relationship.

"The most important business calls are personal."

Do you have common interests? Common hobbies you can discuss? Do any of your family members know any of his? Have any other of your customers done business with him?

Learn dates of birthdays, anniversaries, etc., and *always* send a card – and at every holiday. ***EVEN TO THOSE WHO HAD NOT INITIALLY BOUGHT!***

3.   **Secretaries**

Rule #16

Treat The Secretaries/Office Managers As Though They Were The Customer

Get their birthdays, anniversaries, etc, and send them cards, too. Their feedback can be vital to the prospect in more ways than you can imagine. A trusted secretary will often know more about the business than even the boss. Assume they will be asked for their opinion about the PEOPLE the boss is thinking of doing business with. Treat the secretaries with respect. They deserve it. If you're having a hard time with a prospect, imagine what the life of the secretary is like.

> Sell yourself
> Sell your company
> Then sell the product!

Sixteen General Rules

Rule #1 Nobody sells everyone everything all the time.

Rule #2 Sales is the process leading to the close and not the event of the close itself.

PHASE I -- OPENING—INTRODUCTION

Rule #3 It's not what you say, it's how you say it.

Rule #4 By duplicating a prospect's emotional state will raise his state to a higher, more receptive level.

Rule #5 Present yourself, your company and your product and what you can do for the prospect in less than 60 seconds.

PHASE II -- THE PRESENTATION

Rule #6 Standardize your presentation and how you present it.

Rule #7 The more standard your presentation, the more efficient the delivery and the more control you'll have.

PHASE III -- HANDLING OBJECTIONS

Rule #8 The sale doesn't begin until the first objection is made!

Rule #9 Fear is the motivating factor behind objecting to buy.

Rule #10 The first objection is always a lie.

Rule #11 Shut up and listen!

Rule #12 He who talks first loses. Wait for the prospect to answer, even if it takes three days.

PHASE IV -- THE CLOSE

Rule #13 The hardest part of the process is making the presentation, not asking for the deal.

Rule #14 Choking at the close is going into agreement with the prospects own fear.

Rule #15 You'll never get the deal unless you ask for it.

PHASE V – FOLLOW UP

Rule #16 Treat the secretaries and assistants like they are the boss.

GOOD LUCK!

ABOUT THE AUTHOR

My sales career started by selling restaurant grade steaks door-to-door out of the back of a pickup truck in Los Angeles. I received my Series 22 Direct Participation Broker's license and sold interests in oil and gas ventures, Thoroughbred Broodmares, and coal properties to accredited investors around the country. I sold a ton of cars, and was the Marketing and Sales Director for a specialty-car manufacturer based in Los Angeles.

I wrote financial proposals for a wide variety of clients who didn't have the personal or professional means to either start or expand their business, and then pitched their business or dream to grant committees, angle investors, and joint venture partners.

I've done a ton of stuff centered around direct marketing and sales.

www.ingramcontent.com/pod-product-compliance
Lightning Source LLC
Chambersburg PA
CBHW031554210526
45464CB00003B/1299